LE☉

# LEO

23 July–22 August

## PATTY GREENALL & CAT JAVOR

MQP

Published by MQ Publications Limited
12 The Ivories
6–8 Northampton Street
London N1 2HY
Tel: 020 7359 2244
Fax: 020 7359 1616
Email: mail@mqpublications.com
www.mqpublications.com

Copyright © MQ Publications Limited 2004
Text copyright © Patty Greenall & Cat Javor 2004

Illustrations: Gerry Baptist

ISBN: 1-84072-660-1

1 3 5 7 9 0 8 6 4 2

Printed in Italy

# WHAT iS ASTROLOGY?

Astrology is the practice of interpreting the positions and movements of celestial bodies with regard to what they can tell us about life on Earth. In particular it is the study of the cycles of the Sun, Moon, and the planets of our solar system, and their journeys through the twelve signs of the zodiac— Aries, Taurus, Gemini, Cancer, Leo, Virgo, Libra, Scorpio, Sagittarius, Capricorn, Aquarius, and Pisces — all of which provide astrologers with a rich diversity of symbolic information and meaning.

Astrology has been labeled a science, an occult magical practice, a religion, and an art, yet it cannot be confined by any one of these descriptions. Perhaps the best way to describe it is as an evolving tradition.

Throughout the world, for as far back as history can inform us, people have been looking up at the skies and attaching stories and meanings to what they see there. Neolithic peoples in Europe built huge stone structures such as Stonehenge in southern England in order to plot the cycles of the Sun and Moon, cycles that were so important to a fledgling agricultural society. There are star-lore traditions in the ancient cultures of India, China, South America, and Africa, and among the indigenous people of Australia. The ancient Egyptians plotted the rising of the star Sirius, which marked the annual flooding of the Nile, and in ancient Babylon, astronomer-priests would perform astral divination in the service of their king and country.

Since its early beginnings, astrology has grown, changed, and diversified into a huge body of knowledge that has been added to by many learned men and women throughout history. It has continued to evolve and become richer and more informative, despite periods when it went out of favor because of religious, scientific, and political beliefs.

Offering us a deeper knowledge of ourselves, a profound insight into what motivates, inspires, and, in some cases, hinders, our ability to be truly our authentic selves, astrology equips us better to make the choices and decisions that confront us daily. It is a wonderful tool, which can be applied to daily life and our understanding of the world around us.

The horoscope—or birth chart—is the primary tool of the astrologer and the position of the Sun, Moon, Mercury, Venus, Mars, Jupiter, Saturn,

Uranus, Neptune, and Pluto at the moment a person was born are all considered when one is drawn up. Each planet has its own domain, affinities, and energetic signature, and the aspects or relationships they form to each other when plotted on the horoscope reveal a fascinating array of information. The birth, or Sun, sign is the sign of the zodiac that the Sun was passing through at the time of birth. The energetic signature of the Sun is concerned with a person's sense of uniqueness and self-esteem. To be a vital and creative individual is a fundamental need, and a person's Sun sign represents how that need most happily manifests in that person. This is one of the most important factors taken into account by astrologers. Each of the twelve Sun signs has a myriad of ways in which it can express its core meaning. The more a person learns about their individual Sun sign, the more they can express their own unique identity.

# ZODIAC WHEEL

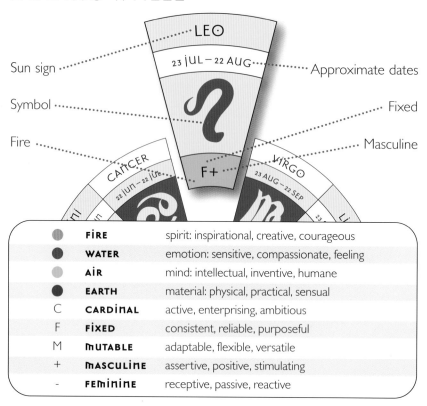

Sun sign

Symbol

Fire

LEO☉

23 JUL – 22 AUG

Approximate dates

Fixed

Masculine

CANCER
22 JUN – 22 JUL

VIRGO
23 AUG – 22 SEP

F+

| | | |
|---|---|---|
| ● | **FIRE** | spirit: inspirational, creative, courageous |
| ● | **WATER** | emotion: sensitive, compassionate, feeling |
| ● | **AIR** | mind: intellectual, inventive, humane |
| ● | **EARTH** | material: physical, practical, sensual |
| C | **CARDINAL** | active, enterprising, ambitious |
| F | **FIXED** | consistent, reliable, purposeful |
| M | **MUTABLE** | adaptable, flexible, versatile |
| + | **MASCULINE** | assertive, positive, stimulating |
| – | **FEMININE** | receptive, passive, reactive |

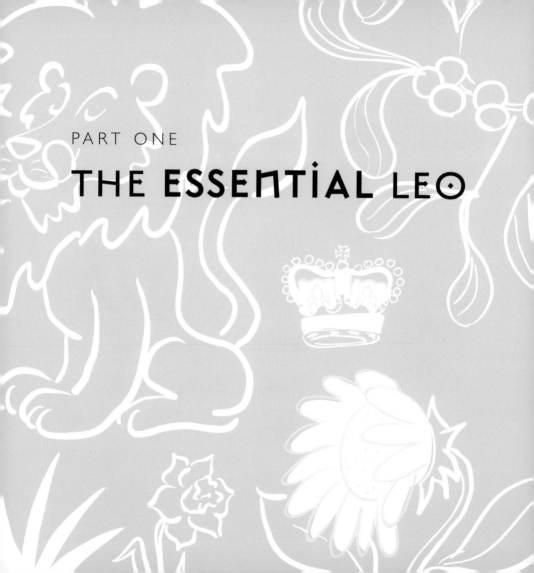

PART ONE

# THE ESSENTIAL LEO

# **RULER**SHİPS

Leo is the fifth sign of the zodiac, the second Fire sign, and is ruled by the Sun. Its symbol is the Lion, representing nobility, strength, pride, and magnanimity. Leo is a Fixed and Masculine sign. There are earthly correspondences of everything in life for each of the Sun signs. The parts of the human body that Leo represents are the heart, chest, and back. The colors for Leo are the colors of the sun—orange, yellow, and red. Gemstones for Leo are diamond, peridot, imperial jade, amber, and tiger's eye. Leo signifies woods, steep rocky places, jungles, grand buildings, and palaces, as well as kings, royalty, rulers, actors, children, and gamblers. Leo is also associated with almonds, anise, chamomile, citrus fruits, cowslip, dill, fennel, mistletoe, saffron, frankincense, and St. John's wort, and with golden and bright yellow flowers such as sunflowers, daffodils, and marigolds. Also the metal gold, coins and, best of all, romance!

# LEO ⊙

The parts of the human body that Leo represents are the heart, chest, and back.

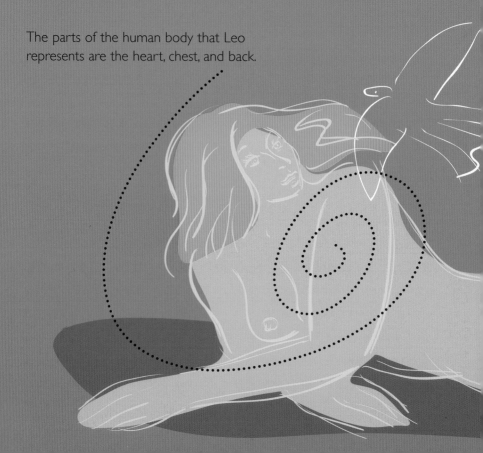

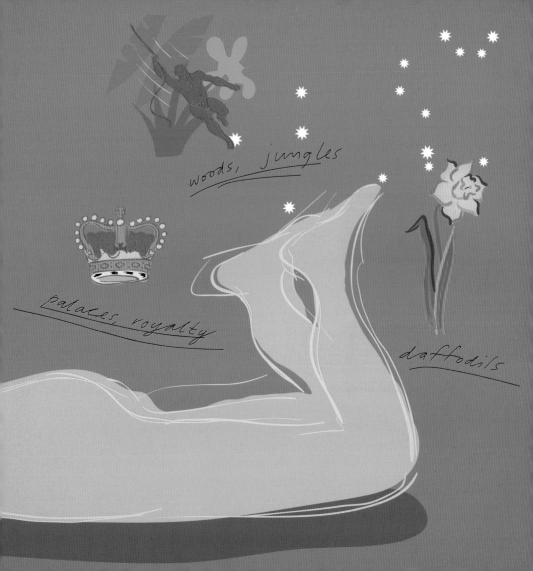

woods, jungles

palaces, royalty

daffodils

# PERSONALITY

Those born under the sign of Leo are enthusiastic, powerful, and energetic, and burn with all the bright heat of a fire. They have such an attractive, scintillating quality that others are drawn to them. Once they are close, they soak up Leo's generous warmth and watch the spectacular display—and Leos always put on a spectacular display. They have a strong sense of drama and of the grandiose and can be prone to pomposity, but more often, they are very giving and noble. They truly are lovers of life and often appear to be larger than life itself.

The Lion, the symbol for this sign, is a magnificent creature, whether in the wild or even in a zoo and whether prowling around or lying stretched out and immobile during one of their frequent and long, lazy snoozes. It always seems a privilege to be in their presence. And that is exactly how Leo natives expect everyone to feel in their company. After all, they're the King of Beasts and so it's only natural that they inspire reverence and awe. Leos are the kind of people whom others naturally respect. They love parties and make great hosts and entertainers, but whether they're guests at someone else's place or at home receiving company, they tend to behave as if they're holding court and others are serving them. They don't even need to ask for anything because whatever they need is usually brought to them automatically. Yet they're not averse to getting their hands dirty. In fact, they're highly creative people in every sense of the word—they're able to generate something out of nothing and they're incredibly productive, too.

If they're throwing a party, they'll happily prepare a beautiful feast fit for a king and will lay the table lavishly. When it comes to giving, they're generous to a fault and don't believe in half-measures. Take them out to eat, and they'll usually insist on paying the bill, even if they're broke!

Leos' pride means everything to them and maintaining it is a huge motivating force behind everything they do. Leo people love being told how wonderful and special they are and find it totally unthinkable that they should ever be seen as just one of the crowd. They're unique and special and won't let anyone forget it! They are also prone to being more sensitive about their own vulnerabilities than any other sign of the zodiac. Embarrassment to them is as mortifying as death; it doesn't just wound their pride, it totally annihilates them. Any people who are the cause of their embarrassment will find themselves on the receiving end of their sharp, swiping claws and may even be banished from their presence. Leos have big, blasting tempers. Their roar is every bit as ferocious as their bite but since people usually know how far they can go with them, it's really very unusual for Leos to make a display of their rage. Big-hearted Leos are very gregarious, loving, and generous individuals. They will happily shine their sunny smiles on everyone they meet and be particularly lavish in bestowing gifts upon those who hold a special place in their hearts. They are also very forgiving: resentment is simply not part of their nature—and they can't bear it in anyone else!

Leos will not count the cost or regret a single dime spent on providing their loved ones with not only the necessities of life, but also special luxuries. They enjoy being in the position of overwhelming others with their extravagant generosity. Indeed nothing makes Leos feel happier or more fulfilled than to be surrounded by other happy people, so they will do their utmost to make others cheerful whenever they can. It helps that Leo people have such a great sense of drama; they can put on a show that will razzle-dazzle anyone. And they love it! It would be hard to ignore Leo's big personality. It's not that they seek attention, just that they attract it naturally. When they walk into a room, the whole place lights up as if a ray of sunshine is beaming in through the window.

Grabbing and holding the attention of an audience gives them a real buzz and when they're in performance mode, it matters not a jot whether that audience consists of one or many. And their material is just as irrelevant; they could be performing an intimate love scene, telling a funny story, or getting annoyed. What's certain is that they'll do it big—putting on such a magnificent display that no one will forget it in a hurry. It all comes down to having a commanding presence and knowing how to use it to good effect. Never will Leos give the impression that they are weak, uncomfortable, or insecure. Even on the rare occasion that it's true, the show must go on. They'll exude self-confidence even if they don't feel it, and that will have everyone treating them with respect and admiration—which will help them to believe in their own charade.

But it isn't unknown to find a Leo who doesn't put on a show. There are some Leos who sit quietly, watching everyone else as though life were a play being acted out especially for them! It's true that Leos can be arrogant, opinionated, and bossy but underneath it all, they are also dignified and fiercely loyal. They are wonderful people to know and love. Stroking their ego is one way to stay at the head of their list of favorite people, but they are nobody's fool. They are extremely honorable and expect the same high standards from others.

## CAREER & MONEY

Leo's enthusiasm really gets a chance to shine in the workplace—if it can be called work, that is! This is because whichever career Leos choose, it must be something at which they can be admired and applauded for their efforts, as if on a stage. This is what fuels their zealous approach to making a living. Whatever they do, they need to find it enjoyable as there is nothing more soul-destroying for Leos than to occupy themselves with something they dislike. Experimenting is one thing, but being stuck in a dead-end job is quite another. When they do find a career they enjoy, they really throw themselves into it. Their level of devotion is such that they can be relied upon completely. They're eager and steady, so they make ideal work colleagues. They're also inherently creative, so any career that allows them to simultaneously express their extraordinary abilities and win praise will suit them to a tee. Although they are highly productive people, working on a production line wouldn't be enough of a stimulus for their big hearts; they need to be building, creating, and working toward some goal that feeds their internal fire—their passion.

Leos have an amazing flair for entertainment and drama. They are totally natural on stage and audiences adore them, so many Leos are professional actors, performers, or directors, or hold some position that underlines their glamorous image. With their robust constitution and strong liking for coming out on top, they also make very successful sports people; the glory of winning is very attractive to Leos. In addition, with gold being their metal, many become jewelers; there's nothing better than dripping in jewels in order to impress!

It would be rare to find any Leos in a subordinate position, however, unless it's a position in which they really feel that their input is valued and valuable. They are represented by the King of Beasts so they are naturally commanding; they like being in charge and they're good at it! It's not surprising that there have been more presidents of the United States and of France born under the sign of Leo than under any other Sun sign. They can get a bit bossy but are so generous both materially and emotionally that it would be hard to find any real reason to complain about them. They have a way of balancing things out: for example, if they feel they've been a little too hard on someone, that person will be first in line for any favors next time around.

Leos' gifts come straight from their heart, but their heart can be bigger than their purse, so they need to be meticulous about how much money they really have. They don't mind picking up the tab; in fact they enjoy it, which is why they really need to avoid going out whenever cash is a little tight. When it comes to money, they're believers in the "green theory"— what goes around comes around. It works for them anyway!

# THE LEO ☉ CHİLD

It's usual for Leo children to show a sunny disposition from the very early stages of life. They are happy, giggly, gurgly babies with an innate ability to make their parents and relatives laugh. And since everyone will bend over backward to keep baby Leo's happy face lit up and shining, it becomes natural for the Leo child to be a warm and loving person. It is true, however, that these children also grow up believing that they are little princes and princesses, with the right to be pampered and adored. Once they begin to move around and talk they do so with style and will always make a greater effort when others are watching so that they can show off their new-found skills. These are the "Watch me!" children; they thrive on praise and the more they receive, the better they perform.

Their in-built belief that they are special and unique may also lead to Leo children believing that they can lord it over their siblings or other children, but they are also big-hearted and generous children. They are full of a creativity and joy that inclines other kids to want to follow their lead. As they grow into adolescence they have a tendency to prefer the praise of their peers to that of their parents or teachers, so their academic work may suffer while they are playing to the crowd. This shouldn't be a problem, however, as long as when they're showing off, they're also employing some real artistic and creative skills.

Nevertheless, Leo children do need to learn that being the ruler of their own lives and continuing to receive honor and admiration after their school days are over may involve a lot of hard work. They need to show a well rounded aptitude in order to earn respect and liberty from those in authority. At any age, though, the Leo child is a lively, playful, and loving individual proud but usually with good reason, and also great fun to have around.

# PERFECT **GiFTS**

Leos love presents! They take them as a sign that they're adored, which they just love, and yes, they are completely adorable people. When they receive a present, they perform their part perfectly; their reaction is always one of surprised pleasure. Even a small token is appreciated, such as a bunch of fresh flowers when meeting a friend for lunch. If you're looking for a present of clothing, make sure it's a showstopper because they like to be noticed, preferably something glittery or distinctive. Otherwise, opt for glamour accessories—a shimmering gold scarf or wrap, or perhaps flashy rhinestone jewelry. For a Leo man, a gift has to be tasteful and of good quality. Designer labels never fail to impress; as long as it has "special" written all over it, they'll love using it and it will always be gratefully received. They also adore anything gold in color—picture frames, decorative objects, books with gold-embossed leather covers, a vanity set—as long as it looks flash!

However, appearances aren't everything. Leos instinctively know when a gift has been chosen especially for them and from the heart, and such a gift will be treasured more than most. A present that has simply been bought for its flash value will probably be discreetly trashed.

# FAVORITE **FOODS**

When it comes to food, Leos can be rather fussy. They're rather particular about the way their food is served; if it's thrown on the plate and isn't as elegantly served as the dishes they've seen in magazines or eaten in smart restaurants, they're likely to turn up their noses at it. And when it comes to taste, there had better be some real flavor coming through from fresh ingredients because boring, tasteless food that's been poorly cooked, under-seasoned, or had all its goodness boiled away will be rejected too.

Leos want top quality food and the finest wines, and provided that's what they're getting, they will happily pick up a tab that would make most people blanch and run to the phone to organize an overdraft! Because they have gregarious, generous natures, people often assume that Leos enjoy large portions; however, they are rather delicate eaters and prefer small portions of delicious food. They're not really into snacking or convenience food, but they may occasionally enjoy sitting down for a drink with a few tasty nibbles.

They prefer a small, light breakfast: a piece of fruit, a slice of toast, and a cup of coffee are usually sufficient. By lunchtime, however, they'll be ravenous and this will be when they want to sit down to a grandly served meal, preferably in a flashy restaurant. They're unlikely to order something they've never tried before, but they may choose a favorite dish that's been prepared with a slightly different twist. For their evening meal, they'll again be happy to eat a light dish, with perhaps some cheese and biscuits, some fruit, and a glass of something smooth to end the day.

# FASHION & **STYLE**

Leo people are well-groomed and stylish and carry off their clothes with eye-catching panache. They love to stand out in a crowd, but also need to be admired, so, while they do love glitz and glamour, their clothes and accessories will always have an air of top-quality elegance. They can look flashy or feline, but even when they try to tone it down a little and make themselves look more understated, whatever they are wearing still manages to shout "Look at me!" In their youth, some Leos have been known to go over the top with the bold, gold, brassy look; later on in life they have the experience and earning capacity to support a more refined ostentation.

These cats love to spend time poring over glossy magazines, tearing strips off badly dressed celebrities, and seeing if there is anything in the fashion pages that could possibly be good enough for them. Whether they can afford to buy designer labels or have to prowl around charity shops for something to wear, Leos will not be seen in the same old thing as everyone else. They may be dressed in the height of fashion, but what they wear will always have something unique and different about it. Leos look good in most colors but especially in bold, warm shades, so they'll look fabulous in any shade of tan, honey, or gold, particularly when set off against black or white, or dressed up with glittering jewelry. And being Leos, they are of that rare breed that can even get away with wearing bright orange!

# IDEAL HOMES

Large or small, town or country, the main themes of a Leo home are opulence and grandeur. The Leo home always makes an impact; it has style and elegance. Whatever their budget, Leos will always manage to find the accessories and decorative touches that pull together an entire look and create a style that says "sumptuous, rich, and classy." As the Leo individual matures and has more earning power, these themes become more apparent for then they'll be able to afford the luxuries they desire.

Elegance comes first, closely followed by practicality. Leos take a great deal of pride in their home; it needs to be the kind of place where a king or queen could call by at a moment's notice, but it's also somewhere anyone could visit, for Leos are charitable and would always invite people to step inside. The visitors may not go farther than the hallway, mind, but they are welcome to stand at the door and marvel at the splendor—the sparkling crystal chandelier, the ornate mirror, the pristine Louis XIV dining table and chairs. Then there's the living room with animal prints on the walls and hides draped over the leather sofa. Leos are big cats and love the drama of a room designed to bring out the beast in them! And, last but not least, there's the bedroom. This, in a word, looks expensive even if it isn't, but don't forget, expensive is the look that Leo likes best.

PART TWO

# RISING SIGNS

# WHAT IS A RISING SIGN?

Your rising sign is the zodiacal sign that could be seen rising on the eastern horizon at the time and place of your birth. Each sign takes about two and a half hours to rise — approximately one degree every four minutes. Because it is so fast moving, the rising sign represents a very personal part of the horoscope, so even if two people were born on the same day and year as one another, their different rising signs will make them very different people.

It is easier to understand the rising sign when the entire birth chart is seen as a circular map of the heavens. Imagine the rising sign — or ascendant — at the eastern point of the circle. Opposite is where the Sun sets — the descendant. The top of the chart is the part of the sky that is above, where the Sun reaches at midday, and the bottom of the chart is below, where the Sun would be at midnight. These four points divide the circle, or birth chart, into four. Those quadrants are then each divided into three, making a total of twelve, known as houses, each of which represents a certain aspect of life. Your rising sign corresponds to the first house and establishes which sign of the zodiac occupied each of the other eleven houses when you were born.

All of which makes people astrologically different from one another; not all Leos are alike! The rising sign generally indicates what a person looks like. For instance, people with Leo, the sign of kings, rising, probably walk with a noble air and find that people often treat them like royalty. Those that have Pisces rising frequently have soft and sensitive looks and they might find that people are forever pouring their hearts out to them.

The rising sign is a very important part of the entire birth chart and should be considered in combination with the Sun sign and all the other planets!

# THE RiSiNG SiGNS FOR LEO☉

To work out your rising sign, you need to know your exact time of birth—if hospital records aren't available, try asking your family and friends. Now turn to the charts on pages 38–43. There are three charts, covering New York, Sydney, and London, all set to Greenwich Mean Time. Choose the correct chart for your place of birth and, if necessary, add or subtract the number of hours difference from GMT (for example, Sydney is approximately ten hours ahead, so you need to subtract ten hours from your time of birth). Then use a ruler to carefully find the point where your GMT time of birth meets your date of birth—this point indicates your rising sign.

## LEO WiTH **ARiES** RiSiNG

The Leo born with Aries rising is a force to be reckoned with. They have a constant fire burning in their belly, which needs to be expressed, and nothing will get in the way of expressing it. They treat life as a game to be won at all costs, and aren't averse to taking a few risks and playing the odds. Their creativity is immense and as long as they're pursuing a project that gives them a chance to show off their talents, they'll be happy. However, they tend not to stick with the project long enough for it to be complete—at least, in their view it isn't. They have a voracious appetite for doing more, trying new things, and creating something fresh even though they may already have done more than the average person does in a lifetime. Their energy is so great that they're always on the move and always wanting to be the best—and they usually succeed. They are naturally independent characters, although they love being around people for the applause and encouragement they offer. Passionate, loving, and proud, they are fiercely loyal and protective toward their nearest and dearest.

## LEO WITH **TAURUS** RISING

Majestically elegant and powerfully self-assured, Leos with Taurus rising are calm, loving, and nurturing individuals who know their own worth and are proud of their abilities. This is someone you can rely on. They're good with money, strong-willed, and a support in troubled times for those they love. They have enormous respect for traditional values and often behave in a manner reminiscent of a bygone age, when courtesy and refinement were admired as virtues. Although they can be extremely stubborn, they're warm and gentle and never stiff or stuffy. They're great lovers of art and beauty, and have a penchant for luxury and indulgence, so they're happiest when surrounded by gorgeous objects. The pursuit of hedonistic pleasure is a powerful motivating force so, unsurprisingly, they also love the company of close friends and family at a dinner table groaning with sumptuous delicacies. Although they're slow to anger, when they do lose their temper, it's not a pretty sight and certainly not one that will be forgotten in a hurry. But most of the time, the elegant yet down-to-earth Leo with Taurus rising is very much a pleasure to be around.

## LEO WiTH GEMiNi RisiNG

With Gemini rising, the already likable, lovable Leo personality is given the precious gift of gab, which makes these Leos not only playful and humorous, but also superb communicators with a thirst for information. Now they can add a quicksilver tongue to their golden bearing, so they'll be able to convince anybody of anything. They're always busy and in a rush and can often be seen multi-tasking—having a coffee, reading the paper, and talking on the phone all at the same time. Yet they still manage to look like they have it all together, which they have! Somewhat excitable, they're effervescent in the way they express themselves and rarely run out of things to say. It all comes down to their love of learning and their need to use and express knowledge creatively. Incredibly bright, cheerful, and positive in outlook, they don't often allow the woes of life to hold them back from carrying out their plans. They're more likely to turn the tables on adversity, make a clever joke about their troubles, then press on. They are full of energy and bounce and can follow many different pursuits at the same time.

## LEO WiTH **CAΠCER** RiSinG

The ambitious side of Leo becomes very dominant when Cancer is rising, but it's not a selfish sort of ambition. Instead it's the sort that enables them to create the kind of empire where they can gather together all those they love and hold dear, for they have a strong nurturing instinct and wish to protect their loved ones in comfort and safety. The added sensitivity toward others that Cancer gives to Leo also makes them more sentimental and nostalgic. They can be prone to clinging to sweet memories of the past, but this only adds to their warm and generous heart, making it even more sympathetic. Although they'll probably do their fair share of traveling, these Leos will always come back home because they can sense that home is where their heart belongs. There's unlikely to be a bigger pussycat of a Lion than this one! With their instinctive knowledge of how to pitch their skills and back them up with sound performance, they're capable of turning their creative talents into a marketable commodity, all of which will ensure that life will offer them endless opportunities to make money.

## LEO WiTH **LEO** RiSinG

The Leo with Leo rising, or the "double Leo," is doubly demonstrative and positively shines with glory and generosity. They're open, honest, friendly, and magnanimous, so people simply can't help but love them. They seem to attract good luck along with supporters and truly are the leaders of the pack. Even though it's possible for these Leos to be pompous and full of themselves, once it's been pointed out to them, they'll stop behaving this way for they always wants to be seen as dignified and kind. Noble and inspiring, they have a forceful and independent nature that makes them an example to all who admire self-confidence and vitality. They're self-starters when it comes to creative pursuits and they have the courage of their convictions, so they'll see things through to the end. They freely show love and affection and have warm and sunny smiles, so popularity comes easily to them. They'll always treat others with honesty and loyalty as these are very important to them, and as long as they're treated the same way, they'll forgive many a transgression.

## LEO WITH **VIRGO** RISING

♍ Leos with Virgo rising are so agile and alert that they can sometimes appear to be as jumpy as a cat on a hot tin roof. At other times they're as content as a kitten curled up in front of the fire and dreaming of pouncing on grasshoppers in the sunshine. They're somewhat more modest than other Leos, but that could be because they have such great expectations of themselves and have something of an inferiority complex. On the other hand, it could be because of their belief that they sit so high above the common herd that there's no reason to show off. The truth, actually, lies somewhere in between. They're contemplative creatures and they are very insightful, tuned in to many frequencies and often appearing to be doing absolutely nothing when really they're just about to dash into action. That's why it's easy to underestimate their strength. At first sight, they don't possess the usual magnanimous presence that Leos are famous for, but once they start talking, it's obvious who's in charge. Leos with Virgo rising are untiring workers with incredible vision—they're really going places.

## LEO WITH **LIBRA** RISING

With the added charm and diplomacy that Libra rising gives to the Leo native, it's easy to see why this individual is the cat that everyone wants to prowl around with. Cheery and sociable, these Leos can be the life and soul of the party, though not in a raucous way; when they walk into the room, it somehow seems brighter. They're elegant and feline, energetic and friendly, uniquely appealing people—a "class act." They exude an air of good taste and refinement, and yet there's still enough of the warm-hearted, playful pussycat passion in their nature for people to have a really good time with them. They're agreeable, affectionate, and truly interested in others, making everyone feel special and important whenever they turn one of their happy, sunny smiles on them. It's impossible to say "no" to these Leos, and this is something they count on—it is why they make great leaders. They're naturally tactful yet commanding. People enjoy pleasing them and, to some extent, they enjoy pleasing others. They can strike an ideal balance between give and take, so even though it's hard to say "no" to any Leos, with lovely Libra rising, no one would ever want to refuse these particular Leos anything.

## LEO WITH **SCORPIO** RISING

On the surface, this combination may appear to be one cool cat, but inside there's a raging inferno of energy and passion just waiting to be channeled into something productive. Once they get into the groove, then there's no stopping them. When Scorpio is rising it gives Leos the added thrust of determination and the shrewd ability to stamp their authority on every aspect of life. Some might call them control freaks and, yes, they are very controlled, but only as controlled as a pressure-cooker. They're the ones who'll get themselves to the top of an organization quickly and quietly. They're insightful and can easily sense who's worth knowing and when to strike, and they're also ambitious, but not in the most obvious of ways. They have the ability to use their profoundly powerful instincts to make radical transformations in others and in themselves. Their abilities are sublime and they can reach heights of achievement that others only dream about. But they're also so full of wild passion that unless they direct that passion into something constructive, it could explode messily or simply leak away.

## LEO WITH **SAGITTARIUS** RISING

The Leo born with Sagittarius rising is a bright and jolly individual with a philosophical take on the world and a genuine appreciation for life in all its wonderful variety. They love freedom, not just for themselves but for everyone on the planet. With a firmly held belief system, whatever it may be, they exude confidence and hold strong opinions on the difference between right and wrong, which they'll verbalize whenever they feel the need—though they reserve the right to change their mind, of course. They're gregarious and hopeful, with an adventurous, optimistic spirit that makes them popular and welcome wherever they may go. With their natural nobility and interest in people from all walks of life, they adapt to most situations and environments with ease, but won't let life keep them in one spot for long. Being free to follow their hearts and tread new ground is important to them. They have a broad, inclusive sense of humor and are fabulously inspiring speakers whose minds remain open to any possibility. They also have the vision to spot an opportunity where others see none.

## LEO WiTH **CAPRiCORN** RisinG

Having Capricorn on the ascendant gives Leos intensity and focuses their attention on looking after their individual interests and those of the people allowed into their inner sanctum. They still possess the loving warmth and generosity that's part of every Leo's makeup; however, now they channel their creative energy into building a sound and lasting legacy. They are industrious, clever, and hardworking and always keep their eye on the goal ahead. They are also capable of setting a large-scale project in motion and seeing it through to completion. The already kingly Leo aspires to even greater heights when Capricorn is rising, so they'll have a certain focused intensity about them. They don't possess Leo's usual happy-go-lucky demeanor, even though they may feel it inside, but make no mistake, when it comes down to the wire, they're still the self-assured, optimistic Leo on the inside. They often have questions about the mysteries of life and spend much time contemplating the answers, yet won't hesitate in telling others how to run their lives. And with their uncanny ability to get to the core of things, strangely enough, they're usually right!

## LEO WITH **AQUARIUS** RISING

People often feel that this Leo is the one that they can really relate to, that this is someone who reflects and expresses their own romantic and creative urges. That's because, with Aquarius rising, this Leo keys into that little spark of unique individuality that exists in everyone. Leos with Aquarius rising are truly interested in other people, which makes them very attractive to almost everyone they meet. Sure, they often have that aloof, detached Aquarius air, which, added to Leo's haughtiness, can make them appear untouchable, but they're so genuinely personable and sympathetic that they make wonderful friends. They project themselves with great ingenuity and originality and their immense creative talent often breaks new ground. They're also innately interested in the greater good and in what will suit everyone, though they also like their fair share of glory and admiration. They wouldn't be authentic Leos if they didn't! The Leo with Aquarius rising has a wonderfully genuine humanitarian streak. This is one of the most likable and outgoing of Leos.

## LEO WITH **PISCES** RISING

There is no Leo so kind and loving as the Leo with Pisces rising. They generously turn all of their immense talents and abilities toward boosting others and making them feel supported and cared for. They have a natural ability for looking after other people, especially those that need it the most. Imaginative and impressionable, they're also incredibly sensitive and empathic, so they often pick up the vibes of those around them and can immediately start emanating their healing energy when needed. With their natural artistic abilities, their powerful imagination, and their discriminating view of how to combine all of this, they are capable of truly excellent creative work. These warm, sunny people have a dreamy, romantic quality that belies their industrious, conscientious nature; they can seem languorous and relaxed even when they're frantically tackling a multitude of tasks. This is one very productive Leo, who is usually the first to help out whenever a situation demands all hands on deck. There's a soft sensuality about their appearance and they often give the impression that they're more flexible than they really are. They want to please but it won't always be possible because, after all, they are Leos, not Pisceans. This means that underneath that sweet outer shell there is a Lion who wouldn't hesitate to put its paw down when pushed.

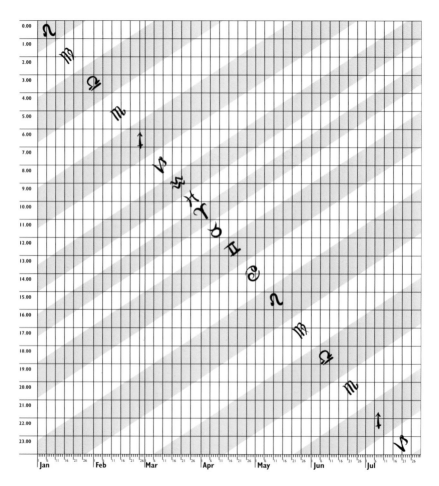

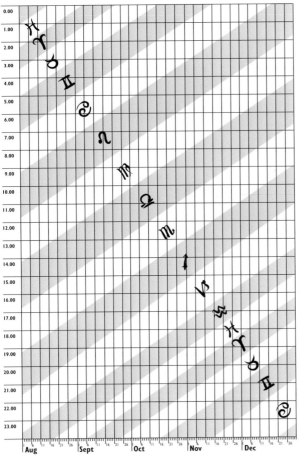

## RISING SIGN
TABLE

### New York
latitude 39N00
meridian 75W00

| | | |
|---|---|---|
| ♈ aries | ♎ libra |
| ♉ taurus | ♏ scorpio |
| ♊ gemini | ♐ sagittarius |
| ♋ cancer | ♑ capricorn |
| ♌ leo | ♒ aquarius |
| ♍ virgo | ♓ pisces |

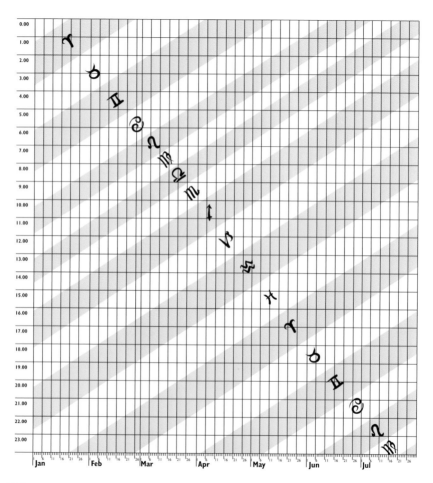

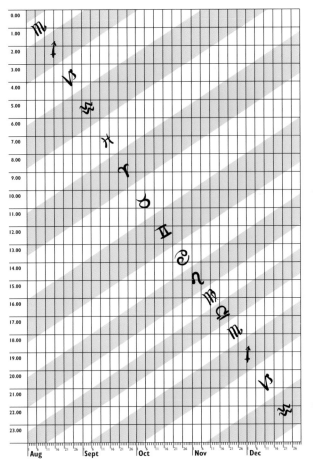

## RISING SIGN
TABLE

### Sydney

latitude 34S00
meridian 150E00

| | | | |
|---|---|---|---|
| ♈ | aries | ♎ | libra |
| ♉ | taurus | ♏ | scorpio |
| ♊ | gemini | ♐ | sagittarius |
| ♋ | cancer | ♑ | capricorn |
| ♌ | leo | ♒ | aquarius |
| ♍ | virgo | ♓ | pisces |

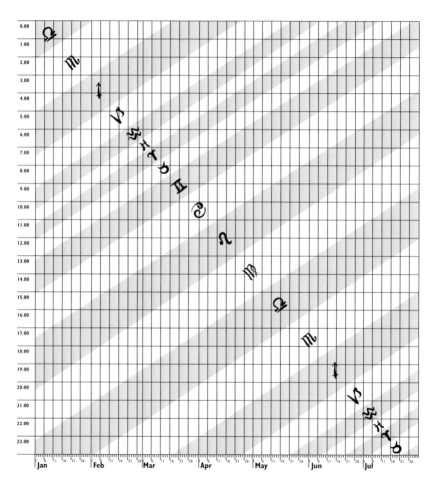

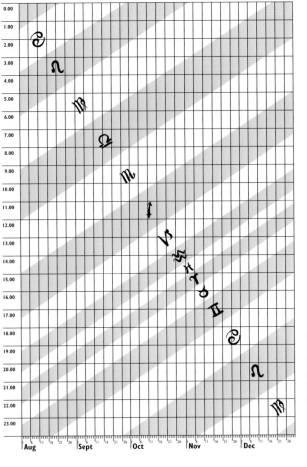

# RISING SIGN
## TABLE

### London

latitude 51N30
meridian 0W00

| | | |
|---|---|---|
| ♈ | aries | ♎ libra |
| ♉ | taurus | ♏ scorpio |
| ♊ | gemini | ♐ sagittarius |
| ♋ | cancer | ♑ capricorn |
| ♌ | leo | ♒ aquarius |
| ♍ | virgo | ♓ pisces |

PART THREE
# RELATIONSHIPS

# THE LE☉ **FRİEⁿD**

Leo is one of the most playful signs of the zodiac; Leos enjoy palling around and warm-heartedly gather people into their life, but they'll be less happy to embrace someone else's life. Just as it's rare for a Lion to join another pride, so it's unusual for Leos to join someone else's group of friends. With their sunny disposition and generous nature they make excellent friends and they have a warm, dry sense of humor. With a Leo friend you can have a hearty, side-splitting laugh and feel a genuine sense of what's good about life.

When Leos first meet someone, they'll flash them a winning smile, then sit back and wait to see if the new acquaintance can win them over. If they find that the person has interesting, likable qualities and a sense of humor they can share, they'll admit them into their crowd. And that's where they'll stay, for Leos are extremely loyal; once someone has won their affection, they rarely take it back, but if a friend should be critical or dismissive, or embarrass them in any way, the Lion will swiftly pounce. Leos haven't got time for those who don't appreciate their superiority or their finer qualities, but neither do they like sycophants. Despite their desire to be admired and applauded, they prefer people who challenge them, though in a friendly way, and who have the same strength of character that they pride themselves on having. For Leo, having a friend is about having a playmate whom they can always trust to be there.

## LEO WiTH **ARİES**

Ideas and inspiration gush forth from these two minds like a geyser. Together, they're never bored, never at a loose end. There's always something Aries and Leo will find to do. These two Fire signs immediately respond to the spark of friendship. The inspirational qualities of Aries meet their perfect partner in the creativity of Leo. Once they find a common interest, they're off like a rocket, but if there's a hint of disagreement, a clash of egos could send their fires raging out of control. As long as they're both willing to admit to the possibility of competition, they should be able to cope with it with good-natured cheer.

## LEO WiTH **TAURUS**

Unless there's the deep bond between them that comes from a shared experience, this may be a difficult friendship to maintain. Taurus will naturally be vulnerable to the charm and grace of Leo and will find their warmth and generosity very appealing. Leo, meanwhile, admires the strength and delightfully indulgent tendency of Taurus. However, Taurus can do without the demands and high drama of the Leo personality, while Leo would probably appreciate a little more spontaneity than Taurus can offer. At worst, arguments could get nasty and since neither takes well to being proved wrong, a battle of wills is often the result. Take one day at a time.

## LEO WITH GEMINI

There is a natural inclination toward friendship between these two signs. They both recognize their differences in character and appreciate the other all the more for them. Leos delight in buzzy, cheerful Geminis with their ready smiles and rapid-fire astute observations, just as Geminis can't help but be impressed by the good-natured warmth and self-confidence that ooze from their Leo friends. Wherever they go together they make a stunning impact, with Gemini's clever wordplay perfectly complemented by Leo's flashy high drama. They know the entertaining effect they have on others and, what's more, they love it, so repeat performances are always guaranteed.

## LEO WITH CANCER

Leo is one of the most strong-willed signs of the zodiac—and Cancerians like to have their way, too. As friends, they'll instinctively recognize the other's need for respect and one will usually yield to the other but both will keep a mental tally of who gave in last. They don't regard this as a competition, though. Instead they both feel enough affection to want to let the other have their way. When they're in the mood for fun and they head out on the town together, no two friends can light up a room quite like these two.

## LEO WiTH **LEO**

♌ This could be a rather tricky combination. With both believing that they are the regal top cat, they need to offer one another a good deal of mutual support if this relationship isn't to degenerate into a game of egotistical one-upmanship. Both are generally too refined for this type of behavior so it's more likely that they'll have frequent bouts of aloofness, with each taking care not to tread on the other's toes. It wouldn't be impossible for these two to find themselves in a catfight, but they'll both be quick to forget and will soon look forward to their next great enterprise together.

## LEO WiTH **ViRGO**

♍ This relationship has friendship potential only if the two of them stay true to certain aspects of their nature. For the Leo, it is always to be warm and generous, while for the Virgo it is to be helpful and of service. If the Leo, however much admired by the Virgo, becomes capricious and demanding, or the Virgo, however much respected by the Leo, becomes critical and pedantic, then the friendship could be a little harder to maintain. If they're part of a group of friends, then these two may hardly ever see one another, but with just the two together, they'll make great buddies. Both will feel safe knowing that they can rely on one another through thick and thin.

## LEO WiTH **LiBRA**

There's a natural sense of friendship and shared ideals between these two. Both enjoy the finer things in life and positive, uplifting vibes constantly bounce back and forth between them. Libra's charm and diplomatic skills are the perfect complement to Leo's playfulness and magnanimity. Both encourage the other to show themselves in their very best light, and when they're out on the town together, they attract admirers like moths to a flame. They make a great team socially and the only other people to get close are those who push their way in.

## LEO WiTH **SCORPiO**

Since both have strong opinions, there could be a touch of resistance or tension in this friendship, which is fine so long as they're in agreement. When they are, they make a formidable team. They'll be attracted to one another because each senses something very promising in the other and, in the early stages, they'll find they have much in common, developing a compelling sense of rapport. However, while they respect and admire one another's strength of character, there will inevitably be moments when their opinions don't converge and then it could get rather loud and painful for them both—perhaps too hot to handle!

## LEO WITH **SAGITTARIUS**

When these two first spot one another, a big smile will come to their lips; both will be thinking "Hooray! Let's go and play!" as they immediately feel a warm sense of fun. Each is good at building up the other, too, though they won't be constantly complimenting one another; somehow they naturally spur the other on to enjoy the game of life in their own special way. Theirs is the kind of friendship that says, "We're great together, so let's show the world!" They make a lifelong, happy-go-lucky pair of friends, and even if they do have the occasional argument, neither will hang onto it or even mention it again.

## LEO WITH **CAPRICORN**

These two could form a mutual admiration society, but except for sharing a certain image-consciousness, they have absolutely nothing in common. Their differences lie in the way they approach life: Leo is wild, abandoned, and lavish, while Capricorn is careful, controlled, and contained, which makes them a rather odd combination. Strangely, this friendship can work if they respect one another and can see how their differences highlight their individual qualities. If they're on a mission together, they can count on one another to uphold their end of the deal and, eventually, they could very well find success.

## LEO WiTH **AQUARiUS**

〰〰 There's an immediate sense of connection, and even of fascination, between Leo and Aquarius. Like all opposites of the zodiac they're on the same wavelength, so things can really buzz and zing between these two. If they find themselves in a room full of people, they'll constantly be looking to one another, not for support so much as for the shared understanding and sense of amusement that is almost telepathic between them. When they're together, it's as though they're part of a well-rehearsed double act.

## LEO WiTH **PiSCES**

)( This is an intriguing friendship, for each will raise questions in the other that only the questioner will have the answers to. But this basic lack of understanding between them is no barrier to their camaraderie because, occasionally, they will turn on lights for the other that will illuminate new ways of thinking and of seeing the world. At first, Pisces might shy away from the outgoing Leo and Leo might be worried about disturbing the contemplative Pisces, but when they do start to talk, it could be hard to pull them apart. Once contact has been made, both will find that they have so much to discover about human nature.

# THE **LEO WOMAN** IN LOVE

Lady Leo is demonstrative, open, and honest, and when she's out and about, she wears a dignified demeanor, walking proudly and looking every inch the well-dressed, savvy woman. When the Leo lady is in love, she can be a passionate beast; she doesn't hold back from showing her big-hearted, affectionate feelings and isn't afraid to be herself. When she's alone with her man, she can be deliciously unladylike and not at all proper; she tells it like it is and will purr and growl until she gets her fill of him. But energetic sexuality is only part of what comprises the lovely Leo woman. She's very appreciative of her man and will shower him with lavish, luxurious gifts—always in line with her income, of course. One expensive chocolate, for example, is a far better choice than a box full of ordinary ones. She loves romantic displays of affection, both when giving and when receiving, and her man will find that she's just as generous with giving her heart as she is at giving presents.

She can play the game of love as well as the best. She knows her part and loves being adored and being adoring. She has an independent streak but also abides by the rules of partnership, so faithfulness is never an issue. She's always loyal to the one she's with—no question—but also requires absolutely the same level of devotion from her partner and won't tolerate the slightest infidelity. Her partner must be dedicated to her and her alone. Heaven help the person who is partner to the Lion and allows his attention to wander elsewhere, even for a moment. Then she'll most definitely be growling, not purring!

She gets along best with men who have an outgoing personality similar to her own. Only gentlemen need apply, but that doesn't necessarily mean a suit and tie. It's more about having a respectful and respectable manner. She's not really into men who pour out their emotions, but instead prefers those with intelligence and an inquiring, stimulating mind and a sense of adventure. The Leo lady also has to have a man with a deep sense of devotion— devotion to her, naturally.

Yet romance with the female Lion is not as restrictive as it sounds. It's true that she demands a strict code of behavior but she also has a lot to offer. She's a partner to be proud of and will always charm family and friends. Any man will feel privileged to have a Leo lady holding his arm. Theirs will be a grand affair with many lavish shows of love. She knows how to have a good time and loves to laugh and play. She's also physically active and is capable of great sacrifice and persistence in the name of love. There are no half-measures with her; when the Lady Lion loves, she gives all of herself and is wholehearted in every sense of the word.

## LEO WOMAN WiTH **ARiES MAN**

**In love:** The Leo woman, not known for giving her heart away easily, will be generous when it's an Aries man who's captured her attention. She'll be drawn naturally to his youthful and enthusiastic temperament; however, she won't make it easy on this flashy Lion-tamer. But once she sees that he's only got eyes for her and that he is, in fact, capable of offering loving devotion, she'll be surprisingly docile as long as his concentration doesn't wander. It's true that he likes a regular change of scenery, as he's very visual, but it doesn't mean that he's promiscuous. She's possessive and proud, and heaven help him if he gets distracted, even for a second. She's remarkably quick and her Lioness's claws and teeth are sharp! But this woman knows how to present herself. She is usually breathtakingly beautiful and has an extravagant but refined glamor, all of which is totally irresistible to the Aries man. As far as she's concerned, his self-confidence and innate leadership are highly desirable qualities and she's impressed by his strength of character. She'll be generous with this man, not only with gifts, but also with favors, time, and most importantly, her heart. And he's very keen on showing her that she's exactly his type. Public displays of affection are not uncommon with these two but their dignity will not suffer inappropriate displays of sentimentality, so you'll never see them getting gooey-eyed in public — they keep all that to themselves.

**In bed:** The Leo woman has a strong sense of drama and will easily keep the Aries man interested thanks to her role play and wide variety of costumes. There's so much mutual admiration between these two that they can have an amazing time together. This sexual union is give and take at its best, but if she ever lets him get away with it, he might just conveniently forget her turn. But the Leo lady doesn't have to make demands. He'll know when he's gone too far—and lucky for him! This lady's proud and lofty manner should have him crawling on his knees. And when they really get into the hot stuff, she'll be so taken with his ardent expression of passion that she'll bestow upon him all the delights that it is within her power to bestow and, heaven knows, the Leo woman is never lacking power. She is demonstrative and he responds. He initiates and she will pick up and carry it on, and they'll often meet one another at the finish. Her sometimes domineering style will drive him wild just as his powerfully masculine and animalistic magnetism will have her playfully inviting him to join in the sport. They may be too hot for some, but these two energetic Fire signs are the perfect combination for making the most of playful antics, ardent feelings, and a big, big love! They'll never tire of each other's bodies.

## LEO WOMAN WITH **TAURUS MAN**

**In love:** The Taurus man can be extremely stubborn, but he'll find it very difficult to remain invulnerable to the charm and grace of a Leo woman. And she is very susceptible to a man with a discerning eye. A little flattery and an expensive gift will work wonders to win the heart of a Lioness, and the Taurus man will not be able to resist a woman who so graciously and gratefully receives his gifts and delights in his charms. He could, however, do without the demands and drama that the Lady Lion, who is a queen, after all, feels are part of her remit. He won't rise to them, or bow and scrape, either. He sometimes finds the glitz-and-glamor thing to be too much flash and sparkle. He's a down-to-earth sort of guy and not used to the fast paced high life that Leo loves, whereas she's a sucker for pomp and pageantry and will fall for it, whoever provides it. The way he sees it, if he's going to offer her affection and attention, then there is absolutely no need for her to attract them from anyone else, for any reason! He just needs to learn that Leo is very loyal and doesn't like being mistrusted. He'll find it hard to resist her but she'll gain more from this relationship than she thinks, so it would be best for her not to take advantage of his good nature.

 **In bed:** The Taurus man in bed is more sensual creature than wild beast. He likes to take his lovemaking long and slow, coming to a very, very gradual climax. The Leo lady will probably be in the multiples by then, but he'll keep going. She's not going to complain! After all, she loves his foreplay and the way he brings her to a frenzied climax. If she indulges him it won't stop there, but Lady Leo has all the patience of…well, a Lioness. Once she has her prey in sight she'll chase him down and tear off his clothes with her teeth, then make a real meal of him. He won't know what's hit him! And again, when faced with such ardent passion, it's unlikely he's going to complain. So where's the problem? Well, they're both stubborn and both like having things their own way; while he wants to slow her down and savor every sexy moment, she wants to gorge herself on passion. He'll find it hard to deal with her continued need for spontaneity, just as she'll resent any pressure on her to tone down her more flamboyant bedroom antics. However, the Leo lady doesn't mind the challenge. If she really has her heart set on the Bull, then she'll just keep going, which will naturally hot up his senses. Once he's turned on, it's near-impossible to turn him off, so even with all her drama, why would he want to try?

## LEO WOMAN WITH GEMINI MAN

**In love:** She's picking up good vibrations from the flirty Gemini man while he ups the energy level of conversation and love around her. The big-hearted Leo woman has a generous laugh and his quick wit will give her plenty of opportunity to spend it freely. There'll be many a playful moment in this relationship as she enjoys seeing his response to her good-humored teasing. He'll fall at her feet and offer up his heart the moment she radiates that famous warmth of hers in his direction because, of course, just being in this regal lady's company is a privilege. He feels honored and flattered by his ability to bring a sunny smile to her face. These two are natural friends and will give each other plenty of latitude to express their unique individuality without compromising, but compromising is really essential when it comes to a Gemini man and Leo woman. There will be the odd occasion when his lighthearted manner can seem to her to be somewhat lightweight, and when her powerful personality and dynamism could completely overwhelm his more fragile ego. She is demanding and he can be flaky, and the more demanding she gets, the flakier he becomes, unless a line is drawn and they both agree on a limit. With so much admiration and respect for one another, agreeing a limit is something that they should easily be able to do. This love match holds massive potential as long as both are aware of their own occasionally challenging behavior, and as long as they keep up the lavish demonstrations of affection.

**In bed:** The passion and heat that the Leo woman can generate in the bedroom will inflame this man until he's like a firework on a clear, cloudless night. The whole bedroom will crackle and sizzle with their fiery explosions. Once Lady Lion gets hot, she burns with lustful desire and is almost too hot for words, but a Gemini man can handle her. He will delight and excite her but this freedom-loving Gemini man is not the type to cage this lioness in. He'll be expert at lighting her touch-paper and fanning her into a raging, rampant wanton, but he may find that he's got more than he bargained for. If he then behaves a little timid and nervous, it's only because lion taming is not what he's trained for. She could make a meal of him, which, it's readily apparent, is a massive turn-on, but eating him all in one go just makes her hungrier still. He could use some instruction and no one could teach a Gemini man how to honor his sexual promises better than a Leo woman. She'll love his willingness and he'll love her need for him.

## LEO WOMAN WiTH **CANCER MAN**

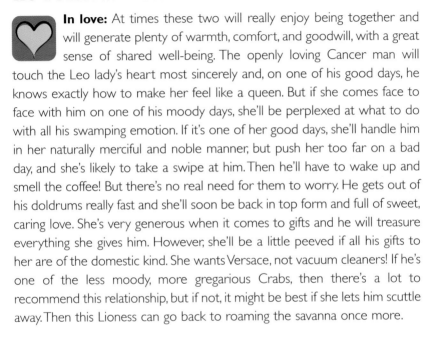

**In love:** At times these two will really enjoy being together and will generate plenty of warmth, comfort, and goodwill, with a great sense of shared well-being. The openly loving Cancer man will touch the Leo lady's heart most sincerely and, on one of his good days, he knows exactly how to make her feel like a queen. But if she comes face to face with him on one of his moody days, she'll be perplexed at what to do with all his swamping emotion. If it's one of her good days, she'll handle him in her naturally merciful and noble manner, but push her too far on a bad day, and she's likely to take a swipe at him. Then he'll have to wake up and smell the coffee! But there's no real need for them to worry. He gets out of his doldrums really fast and she'll soon be back in top form and full of sweet, caring love. She's very generous when it comes to gifts and he will treasure everything she gives him. However, she'll be a little peeved if all his gifts to her are of the domestic kind. She wants Versace, not vacuum cleaners! If he's one of the less moody, more gregarious Crabs, then there's a lot to recommend this relationship, but if not, it might be best if she lets him scuttle away. Then this Lioness can go back to roaming the savanna once more.

**In bed:** The tender, gentle, intuitive lovemaking that the Cancer man is expert at is the perfect tonic for this luxury-loving Leo lady, particularly when she's in one of her languorous, lounging moods. The trouble is that she's unlikely to stay in it once her libido has been livened up and he'll know when he's turned her on because she'll very quickly become a wild cat—perhaps a bit too much of one for the gentle Cancer man. She'll want something to sink her teeth into, so he'll probably end up with a few more nibble marks or scratches on his back than he had planned. The Lady Lion instinctively leaps into action whenever he strokes her mane or ruffles her fur. He's very instinctive and can play the hard man when the occasion calls for it, but he mostly prefers to take a softer, more emotional approach to erotic intimacy. Her animal appetites need a rapturous response, but since the Cancer man's rapture shows itself as calm, careful sweetness, she simply won't understand it. He has claws too, but his are of the type that hold onto her and never let go. He may pour all his heartfelt loving tenderness over her but he could end up drowning her raging fire. It's definitely a matter of timing.

## LEO WOMAN WiTH **LEO MAN**

**In love:** The Leo man and Leo woman are so full of affection and respect for one another that they just can't help but fall in love, but it's not always instantaneous. Instead they might circle one another first, like two big Lions carefully eyeing each other with hungry curiosity. And since both are proud, neither will show any sign of weakness for the other. However, they both love on a grand scale and it's easy for them to love one another totally; it just takes time to know what the other is about. Once they discover how much they have in common, there'll be a natural draw. There will always be a strong sense of competition between them, which can be beneficial but also has its bad side. If, for example, she buys him a present as a symbol of her love, she may well expect him to reciprocate with one that's at least twice as expensive and twice as impressive. Such extravagant one-upmanship can get costly. But aside from this, the capacity of a Lion's heart is massive, so neither of them will experience a lack of feeling from their partner; romance and creativity reign supreme. But what about those boring practicalities that life is constantly throwing in their path? Which of these two regal creatures will step down from their throne to pick them up? Unless they draw up a treaty between them and agree to accept an equal share of responsibility, this love may simply be too grand for both of them.

**In bed:** The Leo man and Leo woman will have a great time in bed together. On the surface, they don't appear to be particularly primal; that would lower the tone. But it's obvious from the way they look so deeply into one another's eyes that there's something very special going on between them. They are playful yet powerful lovers. These two Lions have the kind of astral, hungry affair that might just leave them with claw marks on their backs! They're frisky, pouncing cats who may pet, paw, or even bite one another, but it's all in the name of love, so there'll be no harm done and no real scars—they're just too caring about one another. Both are so full of vitality and have such a strong sense of drama that the scene is set for a torrid and dramatic love affair. Showing off their sexual prowess in the bedroom will heighten their arousal, particularly if they patiently take it in turns to show their ardent appreciation for each other rather than acting as if they're taking part in a competition. Occasionally, Leos can be rather lazy lovers, waiting to be pampered, preened, and adored rather than making much effort themselves, but as long as they're not both waiting at the same time, their instincts for knowing just how to excite each other will have them romping around the bedroom.

## LEO WOMAN WITH VIRGO MAN

**In love:** At first glance, the Leo woman together with the Virgo man epitomize success in love. Theirs is a passionate, yet practical set-up. He'll be very supportive of her, encouraging her in her career and helping out at home, for who could fail to want to help a Leo woman? After all, she's royalty! He'll be enamored with her warm smile, her big personality, her presence, and her sense of command, and he'll dote on her completely. She'll offer him the loyalty and prestige that he desires and deserves. These two individuals could really depend on one another and could make a habit of it. But there's a catch: When the Virgo man wants to assert his masculine nature, he might feel that she doesn't need him as much as he would like. The Leo woman might make him feel like the mouse that her fantastic feline self has trapped only in order to feed her needs. But he's smart enough to stay ahead of the game and could lead her on a merry chase now and then. Her tenacity in holding onto him should be all he needs to confirm that she loves him but, being extremely bright and a stickler for detail, he may attempt to hold his own by dropping a few hints about the areas in which she isn't quite coming up to scratch. That's a very dangerous game to play unless he wants to have his eyes scratched out—Lady Lions don't take criticism well.

**In bed:** The Virgo man is far less spontaneous than the Leo woman and much, much subtler, but make no mistake, this man is no mouse—except perhaps when he's exploring every single inch of the Leo woman's delicious body. He's capable of making her even wilder than she already is, and that's no small feat. His tickling, teasing style is very different from hers and it really turns her on, while her passionate, voracious style will very quickly arouse his interest. Since the Lady Leo loves to be adoringly admired, she may well put on a show to turn him on and he'll be an avid watcher, before quickly joining in. His physical needs run very deep, but her passion is sharp enough to do far more than just scratch the surface: she'll claw her way down to the furthest depths of his lustful sexuality. The Virgo man needs her fire to melt his resistance and to allow his sensuality to surface, but that takes time, so she'll have to be careful not to burn herself out in the process. However, once he discovers that deep reservoir of passion hidden within himself, he'll devote all of it to her service, falling on his knees before his luscious Leo lover and worshiping her regal presence.

## LEO WOMAN WITH **LIBRA MAN**

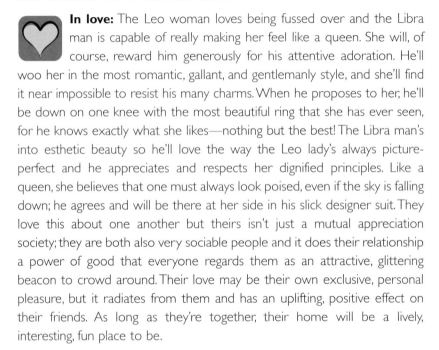

**In love:** The Leo woman loves being fussed over and the Libra man is capable of really making her feel like a queen. She will, of course, reward him generously for his attentive adoration. He'll woo her in the most romantic, gallant, and gentlemanly style, and she'll find it near impossible to resist his many charms. When he proposes to her, he'll be down on one knee with the most beautiful ring that she has ever seen, for he knows exactly what she likes—nothing but the best! The Libra man's into esthetic beauty so he'll love the way the Leo lady's always picture-perfect and he appreciates and respects her dignified principles. Like a queen, she believes that one must always look poised, even if the sky is falling down; he agrees and will be there at her side in his slick designer suit. They love this about one another but theirs isn't just a mutual appreciation society; they are both also very sociable people and it does their relationship a power of good that everyone regards them as an attractive, glittering beacon to crowd around. Their love may be their own exclusive, personal pleasure, but it radiates from them and has an uplifting, positive effect on their friends. As long as they're together, their home will be a lively, interesting, fun place to be.

**In bed:** These two are generally happy, outgoing, and positive people, so when it comes to making love they do so in the truest sense of the phrase. The Leo lady has a sense of drama and loves to have fun, so she's full of surprises, sometimes turning up at dinnertime in just lacy lingerie or a gossamer negligée. He'll quickly see exactly what she has in mind, gently kissing her hand, then nibbling and kissing his way up her arm to reach her outstretched neck. He'll be able to taste every bit of her wild anticipation as she sighs her deep, erotic pleasure. She can be sure that he won't let her down. This couple's antics could make a tantalizingly naughty story, but they prefer to act it out. He's a very active lover, so when the Leo lady is in one of her more languorous, lazy moods, she won't miss out on any sexual pleasure. He'll admire her lovely body and tease her with his light, exciting touch. When the Leo woman's fired up and hot to trot, no man could be more excited than the Libra man she's with. He feels as if she gives him a reason to be a man and he's totally thrilled by the thought of having such a glorious woman wanting his body.

## LEO WOMAN WiTH SCORPiO MAN

**In love:** He's magnetic: people—particularly women—are drawn to him. The Leo woman may not know why she wants him, but there's something compelling about the Scorpio man and she has to find out more. This is a tempestuous affair, full of love and hate, but no indifference. It's likely that he can show his Lioness a thing or two about another side of loving—a bed of roses will always have the occasional thorn. This isn't the kind of relationship that will survive on love alone for, although the Leo woman and the Scorpio man can be loving, kind, and generous toward each other, they can also be quite angry and spiteful. However, if these two have other interests in common that are anything but common—for example, an amazing physical relationship—their connection will be sealed by fate. Fate is double-edged and as they can both be rather sharp, they could end up with a fatal attraction for each other that they have difficulty both holding onto and letting go. No one will fill them with more excitement or sense of danger than each other so they could easily become addicted to the thrill of their fierce, shared passion. It's a tough one to call, because when they are good together, they are very, very good, but when they're bad, it's horrid.

 **In bed:** If the Scorpio man comes on to the Leo lady first, he probably won't stand a chance; she'll simply flick her tail at him and saunter off without a backward glance. But if he sits back and plays hard to get, she won't like being ignored and may just go out of her way to seduce him. It'll be well worth her while because he's no amateur. His lovemaking will hit her like a tidal wave and he can get very naughty, but the Leo woman already has her own ideas about what she'd like in bed. He knows this but, just to build some tension, he might resist. With her passions being held under such tight control, she'll quickly get fed up with playing the game and will force him into doing things her way—and immediately! She may not even realize that she's been deliberately manipulated into just this kind of performance, but if she does, then never mind; she'll put on a show anyway. This is one game that he knows just how to play. They say all's fair in love and war, but with these two on it, any bed will definitely look like a field of battle—and neither will make any apologies for the battle scars. This pairing could either end up as one hot and steamy affair or simply as two people who are mad at one another.

## LEO WOMAN WITH **SAGITTARIUS MAN**

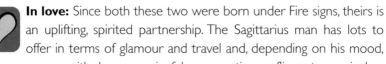 **In love:** Since both these two were born under Fire signs, theirs is an uplifting, spirited partnership. The Sagittarius man has lots to offer in terms of glamour and travel and, depending on his mood, he can come up with deep, meaningful conversation or flippant, meaningless chitchat. The Leo woman will easily catch his drift. They're always on the same wavelength and always game for a laugh together. The Sagittarius man easily falls for the Leo woman's warmth, self-assuredness, and generous nature. Her *joie de vivre* is infectious and he sees her as a glittering prize to be won at all costs. He'll focus all his attention and exercise all his skill on sending an arrow of love straight into her heart and will entertain her, wine and dine her, and love her dearly, almost desperately. But as he's an Archer he hunts from a distance, so he won't always reveal his motives in a very obvious fashion. He wouldn't want to expose himself or let her think that winning him is easy. He spends a good portion of his time away, either traveling with friends or on business, or simply in the games room. He's the kind of man who needs his space, and that excites the Leo woman because she loves a man with an independent streak. One thing that will soon

become clear, however, is that once these two make a commitment, all of the Sagittarius man's searching, questing, and adventuring will be focused on bringing back treasures to lay at the feet of his lady love. Her heart will soar sky-high with the joy of it all.

 **In bed:** They begin on the same note and they follow the same beat, so the Leo woman and the Sagittarius man will always have the same rhythm. At the start, there's lots of bass and the vibrations are felt from deeply within. Next comes the middle—a perfect harmonic connection followed by top notes sustained until they can't stand it any more! Come the end, and they both fall about laughing…then they do it all over again. Neither can get enough; she will love, cherish, and honor every bit of this man, and she's not afraid to make a song and dance about it. This affair is all about indulgence, adventure, and deep sighs, and these two are definitely on the same wavelength. This is the one time that this regal lady's composure is threatened since the Archer really knows just how to hit the spot. He loves to see her lose control. He wants to take the reins and be the tour guide on their next journey to sexual bliss. Only with a Leo woman to boost the temperature can he blast off into the stratospheric realms he's always dreamed of reaching. When they both come down to earth, more often than not with a shudder, they'll have such memories that every time they look at each other they'll be planning their next erotic adventure together.

## LEO WOMAN WITH **CAPRICORN MAN**

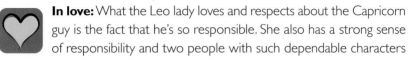

**In love:** What the Leo lady loves and respects about the Capricorn guy is the fact that he's so responsible. She also has a strong sense of responsibility and two people with such dependable characters make for one successful couple. They will love each other, if for nothing else than the level of productivity that they achieve together. The Capricorn man loves that the Leo woman adds a touch of danger and excitement to his life. She does what he would never consider doing; he loves watching her and respects her for being gutsy and courageous. She'll admire his endless ambition, especially for where it takes them as a couple. There will be times when he sees her flamboyance as too showy and her extravagance as a waste, just as she sometimes wishes he'd be prepared to take a risk now and then. She's gregarious, fun, and alive and such a naturally positive person, that it will be hard for her to indulge his occasional black, brooding moods. He, on the other hand, won't appreciate her attempts to jolly him out of those moods; he knows that they pass in their own good time. Although these two are elementally different, both rate status and prestige, so give them some development time together and they'll really hit it off.

**In bed:** It may take some time for the Leo woman to warm up to the deceptively cold Capricorn man, but she's persistent and he's very patient. It will be well worth the wait! She is passionate, warm, and embracing—the perfect woman to light his fire, and once she does, she'll find his insatiable sexual appetite decidedly devilish. This is one very physical and seriously sensual man. He knows how to set the stage with soft candlelight and incense so his lovely Lioness can perform for him. Seeing his controlled disposition, she'll never guess what he's capable of and she'll be pleasantly surprised by his unimaginably deep, sensuous nature. There's not a lot of room for play, however, for he's pretty serious. Satirical humor is his style but if she's willing, he'll be delighted by the Leo lady who can play the part of a dark temptress. Her fiery passion has an extraordinary effect on him, releasing all his powerful emotions and animal hunger, and when he relinquishes control, they could both be in for a bit of a surprise. He will be delighted by the erotic feast that she offers and she should be prepared to be deliciously ravished! This will be a powerful, sexual, and emotional experience for them both.

## LEO WOMAN WITH **AQUARIUS MAN**

**In love:** As opposites in the zodiac, the Leo woman and Aquarius man will be drawn to one another immediately, like a magnet to metal. When they meet, it's spellbinding, enchanting, and instantly intriguing. Her fire and glamour act like a beacon to him; he feels truly privileged to have gained her attention and it makes him tingle all over to have it focused on him exclusively. She, meanwhile, is fascinated by his every move and hangs on his every word. He's an intelligent man, always clever with words, and she'll be a rapt and ardent listener. At the beginning, he'll play the prince, sweetly taking her hand in his and gently strolling off with her toward a blissful, romantic union. But later on, if her displays of jealousy become too frequent, they'll bring most Aquarius men out in a rash, while his overemphasis on the intellectual will have a cooling effect on the Leo lady's passion. Both need frequent time to themselves and really appreciate the fact that, in this respect, they are so similar. But if they have too much time to themselves, they may eventually find their own niche somewhere else. When they're together, they'll always love and adore each other, but if they are allowed to drift and, heaven forbid, fall into the arms of another, there'll be no coming back. They both need to keep their loving bond strong. That way, it will always be alive and kicking.

 **In bed:** It's hard to describe the erotic energy between these two lovers because it's ethereal, unrepeatable, and sacred, but when they get into bed together, it's as if they're on another plane. With Aquarius, the Leo woman becomes an earthy seductress who exists simply to be pleasured, and he kisses her with such ardor and *amour* that her Lion heart races as it never has before. But there are also extremes within this relationship; he has the ability to bring her to the farthest possible reaches of heavenly ecstasy and she can make this often cool and aloof man as hot as hell. Sometimes things can be decidedly cool, but when that happens no one should take offense. For example, the Aquarius man sees talking as the precursor for excellent sex and does a lot of talking, while the Leo woman may view this as lacking in spontaneity—too much discussion and not enough action. However, he never fails to give her good sex when she least expects it! Theirs is really an unpredictable match, but when they get their magnetic vibrations humming on the same frequency, they could have the most electrifying sex of their lives. On the other hand, when they're not in tune, it could take all the power in the national grid to turn them on. However, since he can be detached and she needs the odd lazy moment to relax and recharge her batteries, they'll be prepared to put up with the so-so, because the good is so, so good.

## LEO WOMAN WITH PISCES MAN

**In love:** The Pisces man is prone to addiction and he could very easily get addicted to the Leo lady's presence and magnetism—and once she's hooked the male Fish, she'll have one of the most loyal servants that she could hope for. He'll buy her the presents that she wants, bring her flowers, and behave totally adoringly—and he will adore her, and much more than she realizes. He has a very fertile imagination and, quite simply, he'll see her as his queen. She will love this, whether or not he ever expresses it in words, for she really appreciates people doing what she asks. The only thing a Pisces man ever says "no" to is the question, "Do you mind?" And he won't mind. In fact, he's so fluid that anything she wants is fine by him. However, this might ring a few warning bells for the Leo lady; like a Lioness, she loves a challenge. The Leo woman needs a man who will stand up to her, but even if she tries to pick a fight just to wring a little passion from him, he'll just slip out of her reach, which she'll find very frustrating. He's not a wimp; he's simply extremely subtle in the way he gets things to flow in the direction he wants. There's no doubt that she makes him look good, but he might not always be able to keep up the appearance that she requires from him.

 **In bed:** The Pisces man will use his boundless imagination to set a scene where anything at all is possible. The Leo lady will do her best for him, too, which is more than enough. She's pretty creative herself and he'll gratefully lap up whatever she offers. With love as their aphrodisiac and their hearts locked together as well as their bodies, this can be an incredibly erotic experience for them both. The Pisces man simply doesn't know when to stop: he's oh so sensual that she'll soon be throbbing with anticipation, which is just the type of response that brings out the shark in the normally placid Mr. Fish. The Leo lady is quite creative, and her Pisces man will never run short of ideas to maintain the element of surprise and spontaneity in their sex life. When sex is the bait he becomes a single-minded predator. He will flow over his Leo lady's body like a deeply massaging waterfall and he will often leave her breathless. It often seems as if he's got an eternity to spend with her, which is wonderful, but she has other things to be getting on with and she may have to slip away at times to look after her kingdom.

# THE **LEO ΠΑΠ** iΠ LOVE

Many women find the Leo man's powerful masculinity and magnetism extremely attractive, and he knows it. He'll make quite an effort to ensure that his charismatic image is maintained at all costs; it just wouldn't do for anyone to think him ordinary and, as a lover, ordinary he most definitely isn't!

Every girl who ever dreamed of being carried away by a prince on a white charger who would treat her like a queen, was envisaging a Leo man. Or at least, Leo likes to think of himself as a prince on a white charger, which is the role he takes on when wooing a woman. He'll completely overwhelm her with his lavish, luxurious courtship and is so uninhibited in his expressions of desire that no woman could be left in any doubt as to his intentions. What's more, his intentions are honorable. He has such an idealistic view of love and romance that it would be unthinkable for him to pursue any relationship that had no hope of living up to his honorable ideal.

He may, however, be disappointed a few times along the way, because it's often difficult for a woman to live up to his vision of her as his adoring queen and consort. He also expects his woman to be constantly by his side, at his beck and call, and committed to making her love for him the center of her universe, in addition to which he's into glamour in a big way, and so expects her to look the part. It's not surprising, therefore, that he can be incredibly chauvinistic, demanding, and difficult to live with. Any criticism or sense of betrayal hurts him deeply and if she commits these crimes against him she'll be punished by a show of temper. However, when she's loyal, he'll be loyal, true, and constant in return, and she can be sure that even a flirty Leo man will never let her down. He'll be extravagant in the way he showers her with expensive gifts, for nothing is too good for the woman who has captured his heart. He is an ardent lover, full of passion and romance, and he possesses a powerful desire to bring his lady pleasure. It makes him happy and proud to put a smile on her face.

The Leo man is also very territorial; when he's with her he'll put on a display of ownership that includes holding her hand, touching her cheek, or putting his arm around her so that everyone can see that she's his—he'll treat any man who attempts to get her attention to an aggressive put-down. Being territorial also extends to her; should the lady partner of a Leo man be the flirtatious type, he'll soon either curtail this tendency with his jealous rage or will send her packing. For the woman who enjoys being one half of a "golden couple" no man would be better than a Leo. He'll love and adore her, and will expect no less in return because his generous, noble heart is a gift to be cherished and treasured with the same romantic, passionate commitment with which he'll cherish and treasure hers.

# LEO MAN WITH ARIES WOMAN

**In love:** This is a seriously dramatic relationship. The Leo man has all the grandeur of a king and is someone the Aries girl can admire and be proud of. He's an exhibitionist but in the most dignified way. The Aries girl has all the childlike effervescence and naive enthusiasm necessary to bring out his enormous sense of fun as well as his protective and possessive instincts. They both love the admiration and attention they receive when out together in public, but when they are *à deux* behind closed doors, the story may, on occasion, be slightly different. He requires constant adoring attention from his mate, while she absolutely must come first in everything. If the relationship develops a strong competitive edge, a battle of wills could ensue, and with such a fiery couple, it would be hard to pick the winner. Since both are Fire signs, they deal with one another's enthusiasm, optimism, and passionate energy with deep understanding, and because there is such a degree of acceptance between them, they're able to encourage each other, even though they also know how to get to one another. The thing is, his warmth and generosity mean he's brilliant at making her feel that she's the most important person in the world, while she so single-mindedly expresses her ardor that he'll feel like royalty. This is true love where each genuinely admires the achievements of the other. They could laugh and love forever.

**In bed:** Feeling hot, hot, hot! As saucy goes, Tabasco has nothing on these two. Just one slightly spicy hint of sex in the air and they can barely contain their desire to take a bite out of the other's flesh — metaphorically speaking of course. They're both energetic, if not acrobatic. The sheer physical passion of this union is explosive. It's not a quiet affair. They sense each other's desires and needs and he's generous enough to grant all that she could wish for, while she knows that with her Leo, the more she gives, the more she will receive, and *nearly* as often as she wants. After all, the King of Beasts does like to laze around occasionally, particularly if he's been worn out by an Aries girl. She'll still want to kiss him all over and he won't be able to keep his paws, er…hands, off her for long — especially when they are in the great outdoors, where Lions roam and Rams run free. He'll want to show her how good he can be at the hunt when he's hungry for love, and she loves to be pursued. A good chase is the perfect aphrodisiac for both these Fire signs. He'll be proud to show her that there's nothing tame about him when he's on the prowl!

## LEO MAN WiTH **TAURUS WOMAN**

**In love:** Tempestuous though this combination can be, these Sun signs have certain things in common that could keep them together for a very long time, if not forever—namely, loyalty and affection. These are the basic needs of the Lion, and the Taurus woman will be there to provide him with them on a permanent basis. She doesn't give her heart away lightly so, when she finally does, she expects it to be for keeps, and the same goes for him. Although the Leo man appears fierce, he is much more sensitive than he wants people to think. His pride is easily hurt and he will reward the Taurus woman's ability to offer steadfast love and appreciation with the most generous and warm-hearted tenderness and devotion—all of which will delight the Lady Bull. She enjoys an expensive, indulgent lifestyle, but the showy flamboyance and impractical ostentation that the Leo man finds thrilling could stretch their purse strings beyond even her forbearance. Nor will he enjoy having to curb his playfulness to suit her need for a man with a sense of purpose and responsibility. He can be as responsible as the next guy. He just has his own unique and individual way of showing it. The key to avoiding difficulties in this relationship is for both to be aware of the other's strong will. If they give each other a wide berth to make space for their differences, their love could go far. Disregard the superficial differences, and there is the potential for something deep.

**In bed:** The raw sexual energy of the Leo man is something for the sensually sexual Taurus woman to reckon with. It truly makes her quiver with anticipation, the way he prowls around her with that gleam of erotic hunger in his eye. The Leo man is full of pounce, bounce, and enthusiasm and he is ready to fulfill her every lustful whim. It drives her mad with desire as she waits for this male Lion to pounce. She will play up to his nobility and whisper the most seductively complimentary words in his ear, and he'll repay her tenfold. Leo is a regal sign, after all. He'll smile, or purr, at being recognized for the king that he is and he'll never treat his partner as anything less than a queen. Sure, he may occasionally require her to bow down in front of him but the Taurus lady will happily comply. She will feel like a natural woman in his prescene and will open up to him completely. He will never give her any reason to feel possessive or insecure and she will know that he is, and always will be, hers. If there's any playing around, it will only be behind closed doors and between the two of them, and what a delightful romp that will be.

## LEO man WITH GEMINI WOMAN

**In love:** The Gemini woman will adore her Leo man and that's just perfect, because he'll adore having her adore him. Winning his favor means that she'll be showered with expensive gifts and treated like a queen. But while she dashes about in her childlike way she must be careful not to let her crown slip, and she certainly can't let her hair down around him as he's rather particular about appearances. There's no question as to who wears the pants in this relationship; the Lion is all man and will thoroughly enjoy being the one who provides and protects. But the Gemini woman is no damsel in distress; she'll pull her own weight but will also manage to make him feel she needs him because, for her, he's one of a kind. She scratches his back, and he'll scratch hers; there's mutual understanding and love here. Meanwhile, he's flashy and showy, with immense pride and a love of glamour and sex appeal—and not just his own but also his leading lady's. Out in the world, where making an impact is so important, the Gemini woman can be the perfect complement to the sophisticated Leo man. Her delightful wit and the graceful way that she trips the light fantastic reflect well on him and inspire him to be at his most generous and indulgent. She will be enthralled by his zesty, feisty character and although he can be rather traditional at times, she, like him, is attracted to all that glitters and is gold. Meanwhile, he's appreciative, very loving, and has a big heart.

 **In bed:** Nothing excites the Leo man quite as much as having the naughty but nice and nymphlike Gemini woman around him. She flutters about like an exotic bird, always remaining just out of reach as he stalks her then pounces. The thrill of the chase appeals as much to her as to him, for she knows how to play this game better than anyone! Once he catches up with her, he'll keep her enthralled and her passion expertly caged in order to release it at precisely the right moment. When she proves herself to be worthy of his regal attentions, he'll have her quivering and begging for more. Meanwhile, the Gemini lady is no simpleton: she's quick when it comes to learning his rules and will run her fingers through his mane and teasingly pleasure him with those delicate but dexterous digits of hers. She'll worship him so sweetly that this magnanimous Lion will grant her exclusive rights to his royal bedchamber. The dynamics of this couple in bed are way too much for weak-kneed, delicate souls' or the fainthearted. Their oscillations between hot and heavy, and light and teasing will spiral into a frenzy of delight and ecstasy. They instinctively know how to wind each other up in the most delicious way until a torrent of tension is released like a rush of lava spewing into the night sky. Hot stuff!

## LEO ΠΑΠ WiTH **CAΠCER WOΠΑΠ**

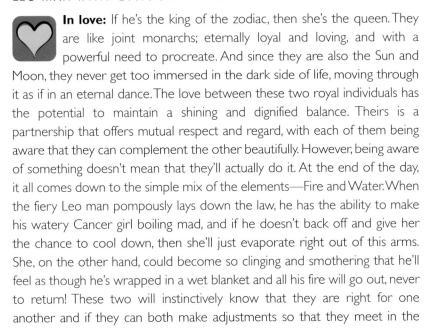

**In love:** If he's the king of the zodiac, then she's the queen. They are like joint monarchs; eternally loyal and loving, and with a powerful need to procreate. And since they are also the Sun and Moon, they never get too immersed in the dark side of life, moving through it as if in an eternal dance. The love between these two royal individuals has the potential to maintain a shining and dignified balance. Theirs is a partnership that offers mutual respect and regard, with each of them being aware that they can complement the other beautifully. However, being aware of something doesn't mean that they'll actually do it. At the end of the day, it all comes down to the simple mix of the elements—Fire and Water. When the fiery Leo man pompously lays down the law, he has the ability to make his watery Cancer girl boiling mad, and if he doesn't back off and give her the chance to cool down, then she'll just evaporate right out of this arms. She, on the other hand, could become so clinging and smothering that he'll feel as though he's wrapped in a wet blanket and all his fire will go out, never to return! These two will instinctively know that they are right for one another and if they can both make adjustments so that they meet in the middle, this could be one magnificent match. There will always be some arguments, but the Leo man has a big, generous heart toward the people that he loves and the Cancer lady has a kind heart toward the people that she protects and nurtures.

 **In bed:** The Leo man wants to be entertained and the Cancer woman wants to be cherished, so, here's a suggestion. Since Cancer rules the breast and stomach, she should wrap a string of bells around her midriff and do a seductive belly dance for him. He'll love her fun-filled performance and will be more than grateful in return. And she need not worry that she's the only one performing; the Leo man has a penchant for drama and he will turn their bedroom experience into a razzmatazz production once he gets into the swing of role-playing. One night he'll be the Rhett Butler of romance and the next, he'll pull on a Tarzan costume and will make his Cancer lady feel like Jane! There's a powerful erotic pull between these two lovers and he can be as generous with his sexual love as he is when he is showering her with gifts. She has a deep capacity to be receptive to the physical love he offers her, while he could quite happily drown in her sensual tenderness. On occasion, when the Lion's being a little bit rough and ready, the Crab may have to put on her hard, outer shell, but as long as he doesn't take her apparent passivity and subtlety to mean that she lacks passion, then these two will get on very nicely in the bedroom.

## LEO ᴍᴀɴ ᴡɪᴛʜ **LEO WOᴍᴀɴ**

See pages 60–62.

## LEO ᴍᴀɴ ᴡɪᴛʜ **Vɪʀɢo WOᴍᴀɴ**

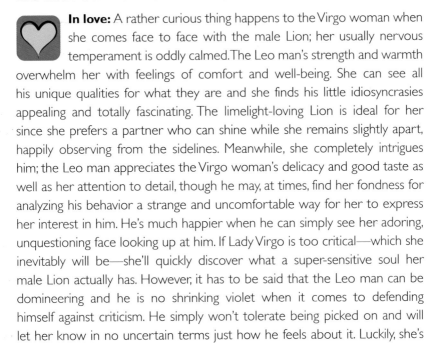

**In love:** A rather curious thing happens to the Virgo woman when she comes face to face with the male Lion; her usually nervous temperament is oddly calmed. The Leo man's strength and warmth overwhelm her with feelings of comfort and well-being. She can see all his unique qualities for what they are and she finds his little idiosyncrasies appealing and totally fascinating. The limelight-loving Lion is ideal for her since she prefers a partner who can shine while she remains slightly apart, happily observing from the sidelines. Meanwhile, she completely intrigues him; the Leo man appreciates the Virgo woman's delicacy and good taste as well as her attention to detail, though he may, at times, find her fondness for analyzing his behavior a strange and uncomfortable way for her to express her interest in him. He's much happier when he can simply see her adoring, unquestioning face looking up at him. If Lady Virgo is too critical—which she inevitably will be—she'll quickly discover what a super-sensitive soul her male Lion actually has. However, it has to be said that the Leo man can be domineering and he is no shrinking violet when it comes to defending himself against criticism. He simply won't tolerate being picked on and will let her know in no uncertain terms just how he feels about it. Luckily, she's adaptable and, because he always wants to be perfect, he'll do all he can to treat her right. These two work really well as a couple—they'll enjoy life together wherever they find themselves.

 **In bed:** When flesh meets flesh the Leo man really is hot property. The slightest touch of his skin ignites a burning desire within the Virgo woman and she wants to get closer and closer to the flame. However, taming the Lion could take some time, and she must take care not to get burnt in the process. She has a delectable physical appeal that brings out the hungry beast in him, so he might be a touch impatient to get started on devouring her. If she honestly shows how much she adores her Leo man, that will fire him up even more, while, if she can open herself up completely to him, she may well discover that here is the lover to bring out the hidden harlot in the Virgin. She finds the ardent way in which he expresses his sexuality to be rather a turn-on, but to really access her own white-hot passion she needs him to take control, not only of her pleasure, but of his own as well. The Leo man and the Virgo woman can really get it on together simply by being their natural, raw selves—he is all-man, and she is all-woman. When they're out with their friends and workmates, they'll walk tall because they have given each other great sexual confidence and deep inside they both know that they are the ultimate man and woman!

# LEO MAN WITH **LIBRA WOMAN**

 **In love:** Every time the Leo man looks at her, the Libra woman feels a lovely warm glow spreading from her heart right through to her fingertips. She immediately connects with his romantic chivalry; it makes her heart do backflips. The Leo man really appreciates her sense of style and her refined good taste, and he feels that it reflects well on him that she's so graceful and captivating. He'll want to indulge her every desire. All Lady Libra has to do is worship the ground her Leo man walks on—and she probably will! When it comes to parties and work occasions, he'll look dignified and she'll complement him perfectly, which is just as he would want. She has a great sense of etiquette and knowledge of the social graces, so he'll be proud to take her everywhere he goes. He needs her vision and broad intellect while she just loves his dynamism. Together they make a bright and lively couple. This man wants to be the center of her universe, which shouldn't be a problem for the relationship-loving Libra lady, but she might find it a little draining to have to continually massage such a super-huge ego. She may also have to tone down any flirtatious tendencies she feels, otherwise she'll be the cause of his frequent and unpleasant displays of jealousy. But his loyalty and her need for partnership are likely to result in real commitment. Put love into the equation, and this becomes a sublime match.

**In bed:** This is one sexy man! What's more, he's charismatic and possesses the kind of animal magnetism that comes from a powerful self-confidence and the belief that he's truly special. The Libra woman should have no trouble luring the Lion into her bedroom and capturing his heart. She's like a sweet honey-trap that will make him throw caution to the wind. Her idealized way of lovemaking is to shower the bed with rose petals and massage him with exotic-smelling oils; he'll respond to this with raunchy fieriness. He'll turn her on with one touch and his unrestrained passion will keep her feeling alive all night long. She'll show such willing excitement in his arms that he won't be able to get enough of her, but she also likes to make a mental connection with her lover, so they may have to take the occasional break in order to fulfill her need for some verbal erotic fantasy. Once he sees how much this heightens her arousal, the Leo man will be generous with his sexy pillow talk. At first, she may have to try to decipher his growling sounds, but once she gets used to his deeply erotic ways, she'll find him easier to understand. She could try to slow him down by speaking slowly and sensually, while gradually working him up to his usual high-octane level of lovemaking. She'll know when he's ready to burst!

## LEO MAN WiTH SCORPiO WOMAN

**In love:** Put a Scorpio woman and a Leo man together and the stage is set for the seduction of the century. It will be high drama indeed! But which of them will be the seducer? It's a role they both enjoy and perform with enormous passion. This is a full-on relationship; these two make a connection physically, mentally, and emotionally, though sometimes it's a combative connection. There is a sense of urgency in their relationship, but they both know that they need to proceed with caution. Each is aware of, and attracted to, the other's strength of character; however, both have very fixed ideas about how the relationship should work and they won't always be in agreement. When they're not, their passions could turn destructive. The Scorpio woman keeps her immense emotional energy under tight control, releasing it only when she feels safe in the intimacy of love. Her Leo man, however, needs her open adoration. He resents it when he feels her love is being handed to him piecemeal, as if to test his commitment, particularly since, in his heart, he's truly loyal and trustworthy. His flashy displays of affection and his extravagant love tokens are appealing up to a point but, without a dependable flow of emotional accord running between them, the Scorpio woman could suspect them of being little more than bribes to keep her quiet. The bond between them has the chance of being either powerful or painful.

 **In bed:** The Leo man can turn up a Scorpio woman's heat like no other! He'll offer her a cross between pleasure and pain on all levels—spiritual, emotional, and maybe even physical. And with her record-breaking levels of endurance, she'll drive him crazy with desire! There's a powerful passion between them that both will long to explore, so they'll spend plenty of nights enjoying hot, raunchy sex. This is one area of their relationship that's sure to be fulfilling. He needs to be adored and she can give him that on a sensual level, but she might draw the line at demeaning herself in outright worship. The need for each of them to be the controlling partner in this union could mean it ends up in a power struggle, but the fireworks that result will be explosive and exciting. The Scorpio woman needs to feel intimacy and intensity, as does the Leo man, but not every Leo man (despite his ardent nature) will find it easy to keep his fire burning when she pulls him into her deep well of emotion. He may find her hunger for that kind of connection smothering and all-devouring, just as she, despite her sensual and erotic nature, may occasionally suspect his animalistic physicality of being egotistical, self-serving, and insensitive. With such a level of volatile energy between them, anything could happen in the bed they share; they should be careful not to burn each other out. It may be up to her to use her superb ability to set the pace.

## LEO MAN WITH SAGITTARIUS WOMAN

**In love:** The Leo man is magnetic and charismatic, and when he makes those grand, extravagant gestures to show her how much he loves her, the Sagittarius woman simply melts. These two are on the same energetic vibration. They really understand each other and, because that understanding runs so deep, there's great potential for true love. He's the center of attention wherever they go, and she just loves to be right alongside him since he attracts such interesting people into their circle.

He's proud to have such a worldly, accomplished, and fun-loving woman with him. Their spirits can really soar when they spend time together and each will inspire and encourage the other to fulfill their true potential. When both have the same goals, the creativity that this partnership can generate is awesome; they make a wonderful team because she can spot the opportunities and he can bring grand schemes to fruition. However, there are a few hurdles to jump first. He can be extremely demanding but she remains unfazed by it, which is probably for the best since it keeps his ego in check—and he'll recognize this fact. Her need for freedom and spontaneity could cause him some problems; he expects to be the center of her world at all times and his territorial nature could make her feel restricted. But, if she gives her Lion plenty of love and attention, he'll give her the universe! And that's what she really, really wants!

 **In bed:** He's spontaneous, sexy, and very passionate—and so is she! Both the Leo man and the Sagittarius woman have very healthy sexual appetites. Indeed, they may find themselves in bed together very often—no matter what else they should be doing. She brings out the beast in him and he brings out the best in her. With her passions unleashed, the Sagittarius woman feels free to be the desirable sex goddess that she really is! And for once in his life, the Leo man doesn't feel that he has to tone down his voracious appetite. It thrills her to know that with him she can be uninhibited and adventurous, and that his passion is as hot and unrestrained as her own, and yet he can still bring out the soft and most feminine aspects of her nature. He makes her feel like a lady, no matter where they are or what the circumstances. She's a lady whose sexual motor is running on full throttle and if she really wants to make his engines roar, then she should put on her expensive underwear, add a dab of her most exquisite scent, and serve him the best champagne in the finest crystal glasses while lying on a bed covered in rose petals. This highly refined behavior will certainly bring out the animal in him. He'll want to devour her all night!

## LEO MAN WITH **CAPRICORN WOMAN**

**In love:** The male Lion will prowl around the Capricorn lady, strutting his stuff and showing off in order to get her hooked on him. And he'll find her a very attractive, trustworthy prey; he can hear her sensuality singing like a finely tuned piano wire that's ready to make beautiful music, while her self-control and physical intensity are like a fascinating barrier just waiting to be broken down. She regards his warmth, refinement, confidence, and raw, creative energy as admirable qualities and she knows that, with her ability to make the most of these traits, the result could be a truly dynamic team. The Capricorn woman is patient and practical; however, the Leo man's ego requires such constant massaging that she may get fed up with always having to serve his needs before she can have her turn. The trade-off, of course, is that he will not begrudge buying her the expensive status symbols that she's so fond of—but she'll probably have words with him about his frivolous spending habits. Is it necessary to buy presents for absolutely everyone? He may not show the appreciation that her satirical wit deserves, particularly if her satire's sometimes directed at him, and she may find his dramatic self-expression a bit too flamboyant for her taste. However, this isn't such an incompatible match as it might appear on the surface.

 **In bed:** Sexy lady, sexy man. And although they express it very differently, their libidos have found their match. Whatever the problems in other areas of the relationship, once these two get into the bedroom, everything else seems petty and unimportant. The Leo man and Capricorn woman really come into their own between the sheets. Here it's all animal magnetism and raw energy. She'll melt at his touch and get fired up until she erupts with pleasure and he's so uninhibited and openly demonstrative in expressing his sexuality that she feels safe in opening up her own intense, vibrating sensuality. This man can meet her insatiable desire for physical contact so long as she can meet his desire to be admired and worshiped. The maturity and sexual authority that the Capricorn lady brings to this union could have him feeling naughty and possibly even out of his depth, but that's a game that both could find arousing. She has a deep respect for his masculinity, which means that in bed, she'll treat him like the king he is and, as everyone knows, anyone who treats the male Lion like royalty will get regal treatment in return! However, she might find him a handful at times and if it all seems like too much of an effort, she may decide to make her excuses and leave. Either way, they'll know how things are going very quickly.

## LEO MAN WITH **AQUARIUS WOMAN**

**In love:** Only the Lion could make a Water-Bearer feel so passionate about a relationship and the fact that they are opposites in the zodiac simply intensifies the attraction. Her aloof but friendly manner appeals to him because he admires her independence and individuality, and he will be flattered when his efforts to gain her attention result in her showing a sincere and sparkling interest in him. And she'll be very interested in him indeed; in fact she'll be extremely appreciative of all his extravagance, glamour, and showy exhibitionism. There's just a touch of elitism about the Aquarius woman, so haughty Leo's natural nobility and exclusivity really do it for her, while he loves the fact that she's totally unique and different from the common crowd. His pride gets a boost when he's seen with a woman who has such an electrifying effect on others. In fact, they both take pride in one another. She inflates his ego and self-confidence so much that when she's not around he often feels flat, but sometimes her impartiality and dislike for the green-eyed monster wound Mr. Leo because he needs to be the center of her world. It would serve them well to remember that they are both very loyal creatures, who want only the best for one another and the chance to express their love freely. Whenever the world tries to encroach on these two lovers, they activate their exclusive magnetic vibrations, sticking together so tightly that nothing and no one can come between them.

**In bed:** When the Aquarius woman and the Leo man want to play about in the bedroom, there'll be some high drama! This isn't a deep, dark affair that's fueled by uncertainty, although they may want to play it that way. It's apparent from the playful, twinkling look in their eyes that they'll be laughing all the way and having lots of fun together. The Leo man is a performer, no doubt about it, and because he's so generous she only needs to let him know what deeds she wants performed, and he'll rise to the occasion. She's an extremely innovative lover with plenty of shocking surprises that will delight and excite him. He's pretty creative himself, and his wild, flamboyant displays of passion will encourage her to show just how inventive and original she can be. Both of them could get into a little friendly competition, showing off their individual talents. They may, after a while, find it a little difficult to keep up this buzzing frequency of sexual excitement but, since he's so playful and she's not unfamiliar with the joys of toys, their bedroom games will continue to have an electrifying quality. Even when the Lion is feeling languorous and lazy, she'll still be able to arouse his interest by stroking him with exotic massage oils and willl soon have him purring like a pussycat.

## LEO man with PISCES WOMAN

**In love:** The Leo man will completely dazzle the Pisces woman. She's like the damsel in distress but this time it's the Lion who's coming to save her. He'll play the true gallant, sweeping her off her feet and showing her the time of her life. It won't always be like that, however. She loves the display of strength that he so willingly puts on, but she's also deceptively strong and when he's feeling vulnerable, she won't fail to be there to lift his spirits. His generosity and warmth will overwhelm her, while she'll fascinate and intrigue him so much that he will pursue her with a single-minded passion that she can't fail to be flattered by. She has what he admires and wants in a partner—alluring sensuality, romance, and imagination. The Lady Fish is rather shy but a Leo man has enough confidence for both of them. He prefers to be the one who shines and she's content with that. Both have their own brand of magic and when they're together, life will feel romantic and otherworldly, but not all that glitters is gold—they might occasionally need to take a reality check! These two could blind themselves to the more difficult aspects of their relationship for quite a while, but eventually, unless they make an effort to stay connected, those difficulties will become glaringly obvious. Her tendency to drift when not fully mentally engaged will drive the Lion wild; he expects her to think about nothing but him.

 **In bed:** Passionate, ardent, adoring lover meets poetic, romantic, emotional mate. Sounds like a recipe for bliss in the bedroom, especially if their bed is large enough to make believe it's a stage. These two will love performing for one another: one could read from an erotic novel and the other could act it out; a dance or love song might be on the program, or even a striptease. But what's really cooking between these two? The Pisces woman brings out the predatory, animal nature of her Lion lover, so she shouldn't be surprised to find herself fighting him off with a chair and a whip, but in truth, she has a remarkable talent for taming him. Her soft, dreamy sensuality most definitely evokes curiosity in this cat and he'll take care to paw at her delicately so that his enormous passion won't frighten her away. What he doesn't know is that she's extremely excited by his lust and enjoys teasing him into an even greater state of impatience and arousal. This Lady Fish would love to be consumed by his Leo fire; she would happily sacrifice her body on the pyre of his passion but she knows no bounds, so even the voracious appetite of the King of Beasts may not be enough to bring her fulfillment.